COPING WITH YOUR EMOTIONS

BY KATE TYM AND PENNY WORMS

Raintree

www.raintreepublishers.co.uk
Visit our website to find out more information about **Raintree** books.

To order:
☎ Phone 44 (0) 1865 888113
▤ Send a fax to 44 (0) 1865 314091
▢ Visit the Raintree bookshop at **www.raintreepublishers.co.uk** to browse our catalogue and order online.

First published in Great Britain by Raintree, Halley Court, Jordan Hill, Oxford OX2 8EJ, part of Harcourt Education.
Raintree is a registered trademark of Harcourt Education Ltd.

Raintree Editor: Kate Buckingham
Written by Kate Tym and Penny Worms
Packaged by ticktock Media Ltd.

With thanks to our expert advisers for their contributions and all the young people who gave us their stories.

Printed and bound in China by South China Printing Company.

ISBN 1 844 43409 5
08 07 06 05
10 9 8 7 6 5 4 3 2

British Library Cataloguing in Publication Data
Tym, Kate and Worms, Penny
Coping with Your Emotions
155.5'124
A full catalogue record for this book is available from the British Library.

Acknowledgements
The publishers would like to thank the following for permission to reproduce photographs:
Alamy: OFC, pp. **16** top, **17**, **18** top, **20** top, **27** top, **28** top, **30** top, **32** top, **34** top, **35**, **28** top, **39** top, **40** top. Comstock: pp. **6** top, **10** top, **33** top, **43** top. Digital Vision: pp. **7** top, **11** bottom, **13** top, **26** top, **29**, **36** top right, **36-37** centre, **41**, **42** top, **43** top centre and centre). PhotoAlto: pp. **12-13** centre, **30-31** centre. Roddy Payne Photographic Studio: pp. **4-5** centre, **5** bottom, **6-7** centre, **8** top, **9** top, **18-19** centre, **19** top, **21** top, **22** top, **31** right, **37** right, **43** bottom. Stockbyte: OBC, pp. **4** top, **14** top, **15** top, **23**, **24** bottom, **24-25** centre, **25** top, **42-43** centre.

Every effort has been made to contact copyright holders of any material reproduced in this book. Any omissions will be rectified in subsequent printings if notice is given to the publishers.

All Internet addresses (URLs) given in this book were valid at the time of going to press. However, due to the dynamic nature of the Internet, some addresses may have changed, or sites may have changed or ceased to exist since publication. While the author and publishers regret any inconvenience this may cause readers, no responsibility for any such changes can be accepted by either the author or the publishers.

• CONTENTS • CONTENTS • CONTENTS •

INTRODUCTION

PUTTING FEELINGS INTO WORDS

EMOTION: A strong feeling such as joy or anger.

Emotions are your mental responses to what's going on around you. When something happens, a message is sent to your brain to let it know what's going on, and out comes a reaction. Simple! If only...

When you're a teenager, there's an awful lot going on. Your body and brain are trying to make the **transition** from child to adult. Your body is awash with **hormones** which trigger developments in your body – but they also play havoc with your brain. People of all ages can be on the moody side at times, but teenagers can take it to a new level! Not only are you under pressure from your own body, but your external world might be causing you **anxiety** too. You have more pressure from school than ever before, friends may be more demanding and parents ... well ... they can be a real pain! You're on the brink of adulthood, testing boundaries and getting ready to take on the world on your own terms. It's an exciting time, but it can feel overwhelming, too.

'I have such major mood swings.'

You may sometimes feel as though your emotions are speeding off the rails, but try not to worry – emotions are feelings that pass and change. You may not be able to completely control the way you feel, but you can control how you express and process your feelings, and how you approach life.

And, if you ever find yourself overwhelmed by the intensity of your feelings, there are always others out there who can help you cope. Remember – joy, love, delight and happiness are emotions too, so as well as feeling down, irritable or downright weird at times, one thing's for certain – there will also be times when you feel absolutely GREAT! This book has top tips on overcoming emotional problems as well as a large number of true-life experiences. Whether they relate to you directly or not, they should highlight the fact that whatever the issue, you're probably not alone and there's always a way to get through it.

'Sometimes I just can't stop crying.'

OUR EXPERT PANEL
THE EXPERTS GIVING ADVICE ARE...

Anita Jardine
Parent of two teenagers and experienced family practitioner. Currently employed as a school counsellor for the NSPCC and involved in providing a solution-focused service for young people and their parents/carers.

Simon Howell
Simon Howell is a social worker and family therapist. He works for the NSPCC.

Mac Buckley
Mac Buckley is a family liaison officer. She has worked in residential homes, schools and family centres for children and young people.

CASE STUDIES
Within each chapter are case studies – true stories about real people who have had some kind of problem to overcome. Read their stories, check out the experts' advice and learn what actually happened in the end. All the names of the contributors have been changed to protect their identity and models have been used for the photographs.

PAINFULLY SHY

HIDING IN YOUR SHELL

Do new situations make you feel uncomfortable? Does the thought of walking into a crowded room on your own fill you with toe-curling dread?

Well, here's a little secret ... while you're busy worrying about what everyone in the room will think when they look at you, they're busy thinking the same about themselves!

Feeling shy and **self-conscious** are really common feelings, mostly caused by those dastardly **hormones** again. When you feel stressed or uncertain, the brain leaps into action – ordering the release of a hormone called **adrenaline** into the bloodstream. Sometimes called 'the emergency hormone', adrenaline gears your body up for action. This is fine when you are exercising, but if you're walking into a crowded room or standing up in front of your class, you end up feeling edgy and wanting to make a run for it!

Adrenaline is the reason we blush too. Its release from the brain is triggered by embarrassment, guilt or desire, causing you to turn the colour of ripe tomatoes just when you SO don't want to! If all this advice makes sense and yet still you just wish the floor would swallow you up when you have to speak in class or answer the phone, read on. The good news is, most people do outgrow their shyness. As you gain confidence in yourself, your shyness should slowly disappear or reduce to a level that you can live with.

'I go bright red and can't think of anything to say.'

WINNING WAYS FOR BEATING THE BLUSHES

Deep breaths
Deep breathing can relax you if you're feeling tense.

Be prepared
Have some subjects or comments 'up your sleeve' ready to throw into conversation.

Don't beat yourself up
Try to ignore those negative messages going round and round in your head.

Ask questions
This turns the focus away from you and on to another person.

Face your fear
You won't overcome your shyness unless you keep putting yourself into social situations.

Start small
Practise talking to family, neighbours and shop assistants before throwing yourself in the deep end.

'I'm too shy to come out of my room if my brother has his friends over.'

But in the meantime, you can practise strategies for coping with it. Try different techniques until you find something that works for you. You might need to imagine yourself in a safe, relaxed situation, take deep breaths or count to 10 to clear your mind. Just remember though, no one's judging you – however much you might be convinced that they are. Most people are much more concerned with how they're coming across! If your shyness is so bad that it's making you **depressed** or you are finding that it seriously interferes with your life, there are helpful people you can talk to. See p. 47 for contact details.

9 CONFIDENCE BOOSTERS: REPEAT AFTER ME...

1 **I am a unique individual who has a lot to offer the world.**

2 **Most people suffer from shyness or some kind of insecurity complex. I am not unusual.**

3 **I have interesting ideas and opinions. I owe it to myself to express them.**

4 **No one is judging me. I've got nothing to prove to anyone except myself.**

5 **I am a creative, intelligent and likeable person.**

6 **I am a good and honest person. I respect others and they respect me.**

7 **I have nothing to lose by trying to overcome my shyness – and everything to gain.**

8 **I am successful at things when I make an effort. There is nothing I cannot achieve if I try.**

9 **Life is full of challenges. I can rise to any that come my way.**

WHAT'S HAPPENED TO ME?

When Nadia, 14, started going to high school she suddenly became a lot more **self-conscious** and shy. It got so bad that she felt too afraid to speak up in class or go into town for fear she would blush.

I don't know what's happened to me recently. I used to be quite outgoing but now I get really shy.

It's got so bad now that even if I get asked a question in class, I go bright red and feel really tongue-tied – even if I know the answer. My best friend keeps teasing me because I blush so easily and that just makes it worse. I just feel on edge all the time. The only time I feel happy is when I'm on my own in my room listening to music. Even when I get the bus into town I feel **paranoid** that I'm going to make a fool of myself and everyone will look and laugh at me. And that makes me go red, just thinking about it.

> 'My best friend keeps teasing me because I blush so easily and that just makes it worse.'

ASK THE EXPERTS...

Simon the social worker says...
It's a shock when your body suddenly rebels against you. It starts going red, ties itself up in knots and makes your head spin. Worst of all, you can count on your mates to take its side against you! The funny thing is, the more often you put yourself in those awkward situations where it feels like the spotlight's on you, the sooner you'll get over your shyness.

Anita the counsellor says...
Remember that until recently you were more confident and so you have the skills to make friends. Hanging on to that knowledge will help you to get through this shy period. Blushing can become a habit and the best tactic is to ignore it and it will go away eventually. Try talking to your friend and let her know that it is really getting you down. Focus on something else when you are in a potential blush situation.

Mac the family liaison officer says...
There's nothing wrong with you. It's just that your **hormones** are in overdrive! Try deep breathing and focusing on what you want to say before you speak. Speak slowly. When you're on the bus, imagine you're sitting in your room listening to music. Concentrate on remembering all the lyrics and notes in your mind. Most people on the bus will be engrossed in their own lives, just like you!

MY SISTER WON'T LISTEN

Jess, 17, is worried about her sister who's lack of self-esteem and confidence is making her really unhappy.

My sister is 14 and having a really tough time at school. When I try talking to her about it, she just starts crying and says no one can understand.

Well, I do, because I went through a similar thing. I used to be really shy and my work at school suffered because I lacked confidence. My teachers marked me down as a low-achiever – it was as if they thought I was stupid because I didn't speak up in class. But I'm now at college and I love it. It was a new start for me and I became a much more confident person. When I see people now they're amazed by how much I've changed.

My sister's problem is that she's overweight and has gradually lost her confidence because of it. She wears baggy clothes and looks a bit of a mess. She has isolated herself from her friends because they are slim and into fashion, and she now feels she has no one. She puts it all down to being fat. I want to tell her that it's not her weight that's the real problem; it's her lack of confidence. I want to help her, but just like her friends, she keeps pushing me away. I don't know what to do.

> 'I want to tell her that it's not her weight that's the real problem; it's her lack of confidence.'

ASK THE EXPERTS...

Simon the social worker says...
The answers to other people's problems can seem so obvious. We can't understand why they don't just listen to us and take our good advice! The thing is, first a person has to want to change. Then they have to know what to do. It may take them a while. So if you want to help them you have to time it right. Be there while they're getting ready to change. And encourage any changes you see.

Anita the counsellor says...
Your sister is lucky to have someone who understands her so well. You are in an excellent position to offer her advice having been through a similar experience yourself. It must be frustrating for you that she keeps pushing you away. Keep trying to communicate with her as you have good advice to offer. Your example of coming out of your shell and blossoming at college will be an inspiration to her anyway.

Mac the family liaison officer says...
Because you have experienced bullying you are sensitive to the needs of others going through the same problem. You could help by all exercising together and eating healthy foods together. See if your parent will pay for a joint trip to the hairdressers, and maybe some retail fashion therapy? Remember to praise her when she makes an effort, and tell her what being bullied was like for you, and how you got over it.

I CAN'T TALK TO GIRLS

Sam, 13, finds it difficult to talk to girls he fancies. He worries that he'll never have a girlfriend if he can't get over his awkwardness around the opposite sex.

It's not that I'm shy. I'm not shy with my mates, adults or even people I don't know. I joke around and make people laugh and don't have a problem — except when it comes to girls I like. I can't talk to them without blushing and turning into a complete idiot. There's one girl in my year who I can't even look at! My friends think it's hilarious — they have no problems with girls and think it's funny dragging me along and watching me squirm. If I don't get over this, I'm never going to be able to ask a girl out. My grandad says that, in that case, I'll have to wait for them to ask me, but who's going to want to go out with a tongue-tied idiot?

> 'There's one girl in my year who I can't even look at! My friends think it's hilarious.'

ASK THE EXPERTS...

Simon the social worker says...
There are many ways you can ask a girl out without talking to her! Get a friend to talk to her, or you could text, write or email her. The problem is what to do when you do meet face to face. We get shy around people we want to get to know. It's a sign we're interested. Don't try to hide it. Show how much you're interested by asking her questions. Listening will give you time to cool down!

Anita the counsellor says...
You are at the most difficult age for coping with the opposite sex. It will never be this hard again! Your **hormones** will settle down as you mature and you will gain practise in talking to girls. And practise, as you know, makes perfect. Meanwhile, remember that girls can often find a bit of modesty and shyness attractive and use your good sense of humour to defuse situations.

Mac the family liaison officer says...
Everyone develops at a different rate. Your friend's hormones might click in next week and yours will settle down. Be patient. There's plenty of time. Why not join some clubs or activities where there are mixed groups and get used to being with girls as friends first. That way, you get to know which one you really want to ask out when you're ready and you won't seem so desperate for a girlfriend!

THE OUTCOMES

After reading our experts' advice, Nadia, Jess and Sam wrote back to let us know how things turned out.

GET CONNECTED

FOLLOW THESE WEB LINKS TO FIND OUT MORE:

www.youngminds.org.uk/youngpeople

A website dedicated to looking after the mental health of young people. Good for information on everything from **anxiety** to **depression**.

www.kidscape.org.uk

Kidscape is a national charity set up to protect children from bullying and harm. It has good articles on making friends and starting a new school.

CASE STUDY 1

Hold your head up

I just say to myself 'Get over it!' I know now that it's down to my age and that I will get through it, however horrible I feel. I want to do well at school and so I'm not going to let the blushes ruin my chances. And I've told my best friend to quit teasing me – as a friend she should support me, not make fun of me.

CASE STUDY 2

Everyone needs support

I wrote her a letter. I know it sounds daft, but because she wouldn't listen, I wrote it down instead. I told her how I felt at school and some of the things teachers had put in my school reports. I then let her know how differently I feel about myself now. I finished the letter by telling her that her friends miss her and that she is making Mum and I sad because she won't talk to us. She never said anything about the letter to me, but I know she's kept it. She's also called one of her old friends and has started going out again. They are good mates, so I'm sure they'll help her get some confidence back.

CASE STUDY 3

Be patient with yourself

Now I've realized that I'm a slave to my hormones, I don't feel quite so bad! I'm learning to laugh about it with my mates rather than get annoyed or upset. That girl in my year who I really fancy is going out with someone else, but I've heard she actually likes me too! Grandad said, 'Good things come to those who wait', and my time will come. I'm starting to think he might be right.

REMEMBER

- Most people suffer from shyness, low **self-esteem** or some kind of **insecurity complex** at some stage in their lives. Eventually you will get over it.
- You need to be brave and face your fear.
- Have a quiet word with friends about how you feel. Good friends will offer each other support when it's required.
- Remember, no one's judging you. Most people are more worried about how they come across!

SIGNS OF DEPRESSION

- Nothing feels good anymore
- Sleeping too much or too little
- Lack of interest in food, or overeating
- Feeling down for long periods
- Lack of self-confidence
- Agitation
- Great **anxiety**
- Difficulty concentrating
- Feeling guilty about things
- Feeling tired all the time
- Feeling that life is pointless

If you have experienced three or more of the above symptoms, and have felt like this for more than two weeks, go to see your doctor. Don't worry, they won't think you're mad! They will have had lots of experience in dealing with people who feel just like you, and should know just how to help. If you need to talk to someone immediately, you may also want to contact some of the organizations listed in the Advice Directory at the back of this book (see p. 47).

FEELING BLUE

KEEP YOUR CHIN UP

Everyone feels down in the dumps from time to time. Sometimes it's for obvious reasons – having a bust-up with a friend or flunking an important exam – but sometimes it seems to be for no particular reason at all.

Don't worry too much if you have the odd day where all you want to do is pull the covers up over your head, roll over and go straight back to sleep. No one is a ray of sunshine 100 per cent of the time.

Negativity is like an illness – it drains you, makes you feel bad and the feeling gets worse if you don't do something about it.

'My friend is always feeling down. She just mopes around in her room all day.'

On the days when you've got the blues, there are many ways to give yourself a boost and kick those doldrums into touch.

Focusing on the good things about yourself and your life will give you the energy to banish those blues, or to realize that whatever is bringing you down will pass and life will get better again. Sometimes, however, it is not possible to cheer ourselves up by doing these things. When this happens, it is usually due to a medical condition called depression.

Depression is an illness caused by imbalances in your brain that make you feel unhappy, tense and worried all the time even if you have no cause to be. If you think you might have depression, tell your parents straight away, and get them to make an appointment with the doctor for you. He will be able to refer you to professional counsellors or might recommend medicines to help you to get over your illness.

'Sometimes the slightest thing just makes me burst into tears!'

10 OF THE BEST BLUES BUSTERS

1 PHONE A FRIEND
*Pick someone who's a good listener, who has a happy **outlook** on life.*

2 MUSIC
Upbeat tunes that put a smile on your face.

3 DO SOMETHING ENERGETIC
*Dancing, sport or a brisk walk in the park. Exercise releases happy hormones called **endorphins**, which make you feel good.*

4 DO SOMETHING SOOTHING
Try relaxing in a nice warm bath.

5 GET A HAIRCUT

6 STICK ON A VIDEO
Or read a magazine or book that makes you laugh.

7 TREAT YOURSELF
If you've got the money, why not?

8 DO A FAVOUR FOR SOMEONE
Helping others makes you feel good about yourself.

9 GET ORGANIZED
If your room's a mess, your schoolwork's a shambles and you never seem to get things right, think about ways to get your life in order.

10 FIND SOMETHING TO LOOK FORWARD TO
It's easier to get through bad times if you've got something great on the horizon.

CASE STUDY 1

I'M ALWAYS IN A MOOD

'Sometimes I feel so frustrated and sad that things can't be the way they used to be.'

Alex, 15, started feeling down when his parents got divorced. Now he never sees his dad. He feels he's got no one to turn to and spends most of his time on his own. His mum tries to talk to him about it but he doesn't let her in.

I was a pretty happy kid before my parents split. Now my dad has remarried and moved to the other end of the country so I don't see him much.

Everything gets on my nerves – my mum, my little sister. School's boring, I don't really have any good friends at school and so I spend most of my time on my own. Sometimes I just feel so frustrated with my life and feel sad that things can't be the way they used to be. My mum tries to talk to me sometimes but I just blank her – I can't be bothered talking about it. Like that's going to help! She gets annoyed with me sometimes too because I am so moody with everyone and don't help with the chores as much as I should.

ASK THE EXPERTS...

Simon the social worker says...
It may be the last thing you feel like doing, but you need to talk to someone about how you feel. If you can't talk to your mum, how about the school counsellor? Just remember, you're not alone – however much it might feel that you are at times. Try making an effort to get to know some kids at school. Following up an interest like sport, music or an after-school club might give you something else to focus on.

Anita the counsellor says...
You sure have been through a lot lately, with your parents break-up and your dad moving away. It's no wonder you are feeling down and frustrated. I think you need to try talking to your mum, or another family member. You might be surprised how helpful an adult that you trust can be. Sometimes in life we have to do things we don't really want to do. No one likes doing chores.

Mac the family liaison officer says...
You were clearly close to your dad before he moved away – are you able to call him up and tell him what's going on in your world? If this seems too hard, you could ring any of the teen helplines and you don't have to give your name. It might be helpful to think of something that makes you feel better – like listening to your favourite CD or writing your feelings down in a journal.

THE TV GETS ME DOWN

Nadine, 14, often finds herself getting really upset when she sees TV programmes about people suffering.

Nadine wonders if something is wrong with her and why she is reduced to tears so easily when others around her are not.

Sometimes when I watch the news on TV and see something about starving children or wars in other countries, it makes me feel so sad that I can feel the tears welling up in my eyes. Sometimes I just go to my room and cry. Even if I watch something on TV that's not real, like a soap or a drama, and something sad happens, I get really upset. My brother says

> 'Sometimes I just go to my room and cry.'

I'm an idiot but my mum says I'm just sensitive, but I don't even want to watch TV with them anymore because I keep crying.

ASK THE EXPERTS...

Simon the social worker says...
If your feelings have started to take over your life and boss you around it's time to show them who's in charge. How you do it is up to you. Give your feelings a regular appointment, a set time of day to be in charge. Go and do something different when you notice them trying to take over. Or think of people you know who are good at standing up to their feelings and get their advice.

Anita the counsellor says...
It is to your credit that you have empathy for less fortunate people. Your reaction is a bit extreme though if it's getting you down to this extent and it could be that your **hormones** are making you extra sensitive. Maybe there are other things on your mind that are bothering you that you haven't talked to anyone about? Your mum sounds sympathetic so why not talk to her to help get a sense of perspective.

Mac the family liaison officer says...
Empathizing with less fortunate people shows you are a caring person. The secret is to do what you can. If everyone did something to help someone else, the world would be a happier place. Can you help your grandparents or an elderly neighbour? Can you babysit for a relative to give them a break? Can you be a good listener to a friend who is down? Give the TV a break for a bit and do something real and positive!

SHE CUTS HERSELF

Steve, 13, is worried about his sister. She has been rebelling a lot lately and has recently started to cut herself. He thinks she is quite seriously **depressed** and doesn't know what he should do to help.

I was taken into foster care with my older sister when I was two. She was four.

We thought it was going to be long-term and lead to adoption. We took their name and everything ... but it didn't happen because of lack of money. Then after about 11 years of being with them, they told us they were going to have to move. My sister became a 15-year-old rebel. She was so difficult that, in the end, they said she couldn't go with them. She went to another foster family and we were split up.

> 'I see these slashes on her and don't know how to help.'

My sister didn't know how to deal with it. She felt totally rejected and locked herself in her room. I think she tried to get the good feelings back but now she doesn't ever smile. She's started to cut her arms. I can't understand why but I see these slashes on her and don't know how to help.

ASK THE EXPERTS...

Simon the social worker says...
People harm themselves in all sorts of ways.
They drink, smoke and take risks trying to make themselves feel **better.** People who cut usually keep it private because other people think it's a weird thing to do. It can be frightening and dangerous too. So you'll probably want to talk to your sister. Get her thinking about what else she could do to feel better. And what help she might want and need along the way.

Anita the counsellor says...
You and your sister have been through a lot.
It must be hard not knowing how to help. Does anyone else know how sad your sister is feeling and how she's responding? Encourage her to seek help from her carers or visit her doctor herself. It could help you to talk to a trusted adult rather than carrying this on your own. Hopefully your sister will be back to her old self when she's adjusted to the changes in her life.

Mac the family liaison officer says...
Your sister needs someone professional to talk to about her problem. Your GP could arrange counselling for her. This would allow her to let out her anger with someone who understands how to deal with it. She has had a lot to deal with in her young life. There are lots of organizations you could speak to for advice. There's still one important person in her life, and that's you!

THE OUTCOMES

After reading our experts' advice, Alex, Nadine and Steve wrote back to let us know how things turned out.

C A S E   S T U D Y   1

Talk it out

I eventually forced myself to talk to Mum about how rubbish I feel. I know it's not her fault that Dad left and she's pretty sad about that too. I guess I realize I've been shutting her out a bit so it was good to sit down together and just get some stuff off our chests. She explained that it's been quite a tough time for her too since Dad left. I guess I've been so wrapped up with how I was feeling that I hadn't really noticed that. I guess talking about it does help a bit.

C A S E   S T U D Y   2

Do something constructive

My brother said that if I feel so bad about things happening in the world, I should stop snivelling and start doing something to help. I never thought there was anything I could do, as it all seemed so far away. But now I'm looking at ways to raise money for charity. I'm doing a kids' fun run in the summer and getting everyone to sponsor me. I still cry a lot, sometimes at silly things, but so what. Mum's right, I am just sensitive. That's me!

C A S E   S T U D Y   3

Break the cycle

My sister went to the doctor who put her on an **anti-depressant** drug called Prozac. Luckily something in my sister told her that this was a vicious cycle. She said it made her feel more depressed, thinking she couldn't cope with life herself. She came off them after six months and now she's feeling stronger and more able to deal with stuff.

REMEMBER

- If you're feeling down, sometimes a night of crying your eyes out can do the trick. But if the sad feelings go on and on, it is time to ask for help.
- There are many organizations that can help if you want to confide in someone outside your family and friends. See p. 47 for contact details.
- If you're worried that someone you know is depressed, the first thing to do is make sure they know you love them. The next thing to do is gently advise them to seek help from a medical or mental health professional. See p. 47 for contact details.

GET CONNECTED

FOLLOW THESE WEB LINKS TO FIND OUT MORE:

www.youngminds.org.uk/ youngpeople

A website dedicated to looking after the mental health of young people. Good for information on everything from **anxiety** to depression.

www.wingofmadness.com

A website that offers support to people suffering from depression, or who know someone who is depressed.

CONTROLLING YOUR FEARS

- **Identify the cause of your anxiety**
  Is it something that you need in your life? If so, you need to confront your fear. If not, try replacing the stressful situation with something else that makes you feel more comfortable.

- **Talk about it**
  Try telling someone – a family member, friend or counsellor – about your fear.

- **Try doing something to take your mind off your anxiety**
  Try going for a run.

- **Set a series of small realistic goals**
  Don't forget to congratulate yourself every time you leap over a hurdle.

- **Look after yourself**
  A balanced diet and good exercise will help you to feel good about yourself.

SCAREDY CATS

TOTALLY FREAKED OUT

Fear is a healthy emotion as it makes us react to protect ourselves from harm. Being scared of walking down a dark alley late at night actually makes a good deal of sense.

Fear is a fairly immediate emotion – we sense danger, feel afraid and our body immediately reacts to get us out of the situation.

Anxiety is a fear that something bad will happen in the future, even if there is no danger. We can feel **apprehensive** about an exam, or anxious we are going to make a fool of ourselves. Anxiety makes us cautious and more alert, which is often a good thing.

18

'I'm too scared to answer the phone. I don't know why - it just terrifies me.'

A **phobia**, on the other hand, is a more irrational fear. You might be afraid of spiders, as many people are. You know that a tiny spider can't really do you any harm, but this doesn't stop you from being afraid. Fear, anxiety and phobias are all normal feelings and none are a problem unless they become frequent and extreme. You might be scared of a teacher and it may ruin your morning but it doesn't ruin your life. You might not feel happy sharing your bathroom with a spider, but if there's someone handy to remove it, you'll forget about it in a moment.

It's when the teacher or spider becomes such a problem that your fear or anxiety doesn't go away that you need to do something about it. When we feel afraid, anxious or apprehensive there can be physical symptoms attached to the feeling, such as: a headache, muscle tension, feeling sick, tightness in the chest, sweating and disturbed sleep patterns. It can also trigger feelings of confusion and **depression**. Recognizing the symptoms of an anxiety disorder is the first step to tackling the problem. You need to seek the advice of your local GP or a mental health professional if your anxiety levels feel so extreme that they are interfering with school, relationships and social activities.

'My palms start sweating and I can't concentrate on reading the exam paper.'

8 RELAXATION AND SLEEP TECHNIQUES

1 LISTEN TO CALMING MUSIC

2 LEARN **MEDITATION** OR YOGA
(borrow a book from the library or enrol in a class)

3 EXERCISE REGULARLY

4 PRACTISE POSITIVE SELF-TALK
e.g. 'this will soon be over'

5 TRY REPLACING COFFEE,
tea and soft drinks with herbal teas like chamomile or St John's Wort

6 GET SOME INFORMATION
from your doctor about sleep and relaxation techniques

7 EXPLORE ALTERNATIVE THERAPIES
that help with stress, such as aromatherapy or homeopathy

8 ASK A FRIEND TO GIVE YOU A MASSAGE
(and you can return the favour)

CASE STUDY 1

HORROR MOVIE HORROR

Kelly, 15, gets anxious when she watches a horror movie. They make her lie awake half the night. She will do anything to avoid being in the room for the scariest bits.

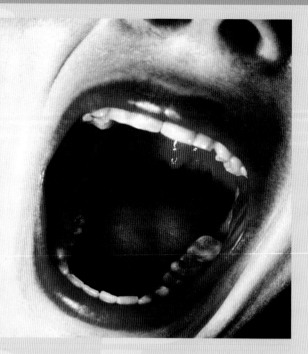

I can't watch horror movies at all. I feel really scared of ghosts and if I watch a spooky film, I won't sleep for about two weeks.

> 'If I've watched something scary on TV, I won't let myself go to sleep.'

I don't know why I feel like that. It's not as if I've ever seen a ghost and I'm not even sure if I believe they're real, but the whole idea makes me anxious. If I've watched something scary on TV, I won't let myself go to sleep.

I leave the light on and lie there until I can't keep my eyes open anymore, sometimes until three or four in the morning. I try to avoid watching scary stuff, but some of my mates really like that sort of thing and I don't want to seem like a wimp. When the really scary music starts, I just go and make the drinks or go to the loo for ages!

ASK THE EXPERTS...

Simon the social worker says...
It's not surprising that horror movies bother you. They're meant to be scary! It's a nuisance that your mates like them. But even if you have to stay in the room because people insist on watching them, you can do something else. Sing to yourself under your breath, read a book or avert your eyes a little to look out the window during the scariest parts.

Anita the counsellor says...
Which is worse, seeming like a wimp or losing two weeks sleep? Some people are more sensitive than others and don't like to watch deliberately unpleasant films. It's most likely that your friends will grow out of this phase of watching scary movies after a while. Can you suggest something more humorous or light-hearted? Make it a policy not to let anyone influence you to do anything you're not happy about.

Mac the family liaison officer says...
Lots of people don't like horror movies. Others don't like snakes but nobody says they have to adopt one as a pet! If you don't like horror films, don't watch them. Suggest something you'd prefer, like a comedy or an adventure movie. Suggest to your mates that you go out more and do other things. If you say 'no' to things you don't like, your friends will think you're being assertive, not a wimp.

• SCAREDY CATS • SCAREDY CATS •

I AM A TEENAGE WORRIER

Bethany, 15, finds herself getting worked up about things to such a degree that she can't sleep. Then she gets anxious about not sleeping.

I get scared of exams and stuff. I get so worked up that I lose sleep. I keep getting my mum up in the night about things that are worrying me.

I used to share a room with my sister but then she moved into my eldest sister's room when she left home. It's funny because I wasn't anxious about being on my own, but when it happened I felt really weird. Suddenly I was aware that I was alone. I do try to go to sleep but I get worried about not sleeping and then that keeps me awake! In the end I get in a panic. I'm in such a state that I have to wake up my mum at four o'clock in the morning, knowing I've got to be up at seven for school.

> 'I do try to go to sleep but I get worried about not sleeping and then that keeps me awake!'

ASK THE EXPERTS...

Simon the social worker says...
Some people love the challenge of an exam. For others they're a nightmare. Stress is great when it helps you do your best. Too much makes you feel worse. So remind yourself of times when you did something really well under pressure. Get to know just how much stress you need to succeed. Let it help you when you need it. Give it a break and pamper yourself when it all starts to get too much.

Anita the counsellor says...
You are at a stage of life where you are getting less dependant on members of your family. You've been through changes that make you need more reassurance from mum at the moment. This happens to a lot of people and you will get through it. Talking to someone about the changes could help and you may find techniques for relaxing and getting to sleep helpful.

Mac the family liaison officer says...
Sort yourself out a schedule – supper, exam prep, warm bubble bath, sort your stuff for the morning and go to bed. Lie on your back and consciously relax every part of your body. Breathe deeply. Think about times you've laughed until your sides split. Tell yourself, 'It's all okay. I'm safe at home.' If all that doesn't help, there are organizations to contact for further advice on panic attacks – see p. 47.

CASE STUDY 3

SCARED OF THE BULLY

Stan, 14, is terrified of being hassled by the school bully. The fear of bumping into this guy is really starting to dominate Stan's day-to-day life.

I'm really scared of this boy at school. He's in the same year as me but he's quite a bit bigger and a pretty good fighter.

He's basically a bully and, although I've escaped his notice so far, I'm completely **paranoid** I'll be next and I just don't think I'll be able to handle it. I change my route round the school sometimes to avoid him and I've even missed out on lunch and

> 'I've even missed out on lunch and stuff because he's been there.'

stuff because he's been there. I'm okay if I'm with my mates but if I'm ever on my own and he's around I'm really anxious that he'll pick a fight with me over something. I haven't told anyone about being afraid of him because I don't want people to think I'm a wuss. None of my mates seem that bothered about him. I guess it's just my problem.

ASK THE EXPERTS...

Simon the social worker says...
It makes perfect sense to keep away from bullies and stay with your mates.
Try out different ways of looking after yourself. Bullies like an audience but they don't like groups of friends who stick together. Think who you'd want on your team before the school bully turns on you. Start building your team now so you're ready for the worst.

Anita the counsellor says...
This boy hasn't picked on you yet so don't let your worries get out of proportion. Remember, bullies will pick on those who appear less confident.
Focus on the things you are good at to build up your **self-esteem**. You have avoidance strategies up your sleeve should you need them and mates to back you up but if you walk tall, chances are you won't need them.

Mac the family liaison officer says...
Don't hang around in unsupervised areas. Keep with your friends.
Talk to someone you trust about how you feel. Don't behave like a willing target. Put your shoulders back and stand tall. Look people in the eye and concentrate on sounding confident and friendly. Practise some assertive responses you can give in case he bothers you. If a problem does occur, then tell someone and get help at once.

THE OUTCOMES

After reading our experts' advice, Kelly, Bethany and Stan wrote back to let us know how things turned out.

GET CONNECTED

FOLLOW THESE WEB LINKS TO FIND OUT MORE:

www.youngminds.org.uk/ youngpeople

A website dedicated to looking after the mental health of young people. Good for information on everything from anxiety to **depression**.

www.kidscape.org.uk

Kidscape is a national charity set up to protect children from bullying and harm. It has good articles on making friends and starting a new school.

CASE STUDY 1

Speak up for yourself!

I realized I was being pretty weak about handling this thing with my friends and horror movies. Of course – like everyone else, I have the right to my own opinion. So, I started saying, 'nah – I don't really fancy a horror movie. I don't really enjoy them.' And the amazing thing was, my friend Elise said she didn't really like them either! So the last couple of times, we've rented a comedy.

CASE STUDY 2

Breathe ... and relax

My mum decided to take me to this lady relaxation specialist. She basically helps people who are feeling really anxious by teaching them breathing exercises and stuff. She taught me some breathing and muscle-relaxing exercises I can do when I'm lying in bed, and also some visualization things I can do to try and clear all the worries from my mind. It's good to have something to focus on when I'm lying there for hours not able to sleep but I guess I'm a natual worrier so it's hard. My mum is being really supportive though. I'm lucky to have her.

CASE STUDY 3

Don't be a victim

Even though I'd escaped the bully's notice, I realized that I was behaving as if I was being bullied. I now just try to stay confident, but keep my head down when he's around. I still feel anxious, but do my best not to show it.

REMEMBER

- There is lots of information around about different techniques you can try for dealing with **anxiety**. Try getting some tips from your doctor, the Internet or your local library.
- Stay healthy – try to maintain a balanced diet and get lots of exercise.
- Try to get enough sleep. Being tired adds to stress levels.
- Talk to a parent, other family member or school counsellor about your anxiety problem. Ask them to help you identify if your fear is normal or irrational.
- Look into a course of **meditation**, massage, aromatherapy or yoga – something you can practice in your own time that helps relieve the stress.
- Listen to calming music or start recording your feelings in a journal.

10 REASONS YOU MIGHT FEEL ENVY

IT IS COMMON TO FEEL JEALOUS OR ENVIOUS OF FRIENDS IF THEY:

1 Are richer than you

2 Are better-looking than you

3 Have a better body shape than you

4 Are more popular than you

5 Have a boyfriend/girlfriend

6 Have cooler parents than you

7 Are allowed out more often than you

8 Go on better holidays than you

9 Wear trendier clothes than you

10 Are funnier than you

JEALOUSY AND ENVY

TEEN ANGST

When you are growing up, it is quite normal to feel unhappy with your life. Especially when friends seem to have more going for them than you.

Everyone gets jealous or envious at some time in their lives. It is quite natural when you spend a lot of time with someone who is better-looking, has more friends or is richer than you — to take a look at your own situation and compare it negatively to theirs.

When you reach your teens, there are many situations that can make you feel **inferior**. You may have a best friend who hogs all the attention from the opposite sex, particularly if you are single. If one of your best friends suddenly gets a serious boyfriend or girlfriend, it can stir up unpleasant emotions inside you. Against your better judgement, you may start talking behind their back because of feelings of envy or jealousy that you can't keep under control. If you are used to spending most of your time with your friend, and suddenly this time is dramatically reduced because of this 'intruder', your feelings are natural and understandable.

'Why is she so good at everything? It's as if she doesn't even need to try.'

However, it is not fair to take it out on your friend. The best way to cope with such a situation is to try to spend more time with other people. Broaden your own social circle, and you will probably find these feelings of jealousy and envy melt away.

Alternatively, if you are the one with a new boyfriend or girlfriend, you might be on the receiving end of the evil eye. If this is the case, don't fret. Look at it from their point of view. They may feel that you are hogging all their mate's time. If this is the case, try to set aside a day when they can see their friends and you can see yours. Spend some time with your other half's group too and, in time, they should come to accept you.

Another major cause of envy is image. When you reach your teens, having the latest mobile phone or designer clothes might seem really important. If one of your friends always seems to have the latest gear, while you are struggling to afford last season's styles, you are bound to feel a bit inferior. When this happens, remember that what is inside is far more important than what you wear or what kind of phone you've got.

'She doesn't want to know me now that she has a boyfriend. I can't stand him.'

5 WAYS TO STOP FEELING ENVIOUS

Feeling envious of others is not a nice feeling. Try these simple tips below to get rid of your jealousy:

1 **MAKE A LIST**
of all the people who you are close to, and think about why they like being with you.

2 **TALK TO YOUR PARENTS**
about how you are feeling.

3 **TALK TO A DIFFERENT FRIEND ABOUT YOUR JEALOUS FEELINGS**
if they are a good friend, they will be able to reel off your unique qualities.

4 **ARRANGE A GET-TOGETHER WITH ALL YOUR FRIENDS**
parties are guaranteed to make you feel better about yourself!

5 **TRY AND SPEND MORE TIME WITH OTHER FRIENDS**
rather than concentrating on one best friend. That way, you won't be constantly comparing yourself to one person.

I'M IN HER SHADOW

Natalie, 14, is feeling jealous and angry towards her friend Louise. Louise always seems to get the boys, while Natalie is left on her own.

I have been friends with this girl called Louise for years and years. We both went to the same primary school, and our houses are on the same street.

> 'A group of girls at school are always slagging her off, and I have started joining in.'

I've always looked quite young for my age, while Louise has suddenly started to change quite quickly. She has grown her hair long and has quite big breasts. When we were at primary school, we both had a few boyfriends, but now Louise gets all the attention. She gets boys coming up to her during break and asking her out, and at the school disco. I have always really liked Louise, but now I am starting to resent her. A group of girls at school are always slagging her off, and I am ashamed to say I have started joining in. It's just not fair that Louise is so popular. She deserves to be brought down to earth a bit.

ASK THE EXPERTS...

Simon the social worker says...
When boys and girls start fancying each other, life gets more complicated. It is quite natural that you should feel envious of all the attention Louise is getting. That is a normal part of growing up. But don't take it out on her — it is not her fault she is so popular. Concentrate on your own good points, chat to Louise about how you feel and these horrible feelings should disappear with time.

Anita the counsellor says...
This sounds like a classic problem of teenage life. In an ideal world, we'd all get equal attention from the opposite sex, but unfortunately things just aren't like that. Louise sounds like an early developer, but you will catch up with her — just give it time. In the meantime, broaden your circle of friends so you are hanging out with people that don't make you feel inferior, but don't cut yourself off totally from Louise.

Mac the family liaison officer says...
It is natural to compare yourself to your friends. Unfortunately, this sometimes makes you feel inferior. This is what has happened with you and Louise. Instead of feeling envious of her, however, why not use her popularity with boys to your advantage? She is bound to know lots of attractive boys who will probably be just as interested in you. Maybe she could fix you up with one of them?

HE'S SO RICH AND TRENDY

Dan, 13, is friends with Rupert, also 13. They became friends after playing in the school football team together. But while Dan lives with his mum and three brothers, and money is tight, life for Rupert is very different.

I've always been really into football. I'm quite good at it and I love the social side of it too. Playing in the school team is how I met Rupert. He's not the type of kid I'd normally be friends with, but we have the same sense of humour and just clicked I guess.

The thing is though, sometimes Rupert makes me feel a bit **inferior**. He lives in this huge house in the poshest street in town, and is always wearing the latest designer gear. He doesn't have to work for his money – his parents give him such a hefty allowance every week that he can basically buy

> 'He doesn't have to work for his money – his parents give him such a hefty allowance.'

anything he wants. Since Mum and Dad split up, I live at home with just Mum and my brothers. We never have much money as Mum only works part-time. There is just no way I can afford the latest gear or a phone like Rupert can. Maybe I should just avoid hanging out with him.

ASK THE EXPERTS...

Simon the social worker says...
At secondary school, we often feel very **competitive with our friends.** When these friends have a lot more money than we do, life becomes difficult. There is no way you can compete with Rupert in terms of wearing the latest labels, but you can carve your own style without spending lots of money. Think about what made Rupert want to be friends with you — he must have thought you were pretty cool to hang out with.

Anita the counsellor says...
When the rest of our friends have more money than we do, it is natural to feel **envious.** The thing is, money doesn't make you cool – it's what is inside you and your attitude that make you somebody other people want to hang out with. Instead of trying to compete with Rupert and his mates, develop your own style and sense of cool, and they will admire you for it.

Mac the family liaison officer says...
Money, money, money – **it's a problem throughout most people's lives.** It is only natural that hanging out with Rupert and his friends makes you want the latest things to fit in. But try and understand the position your mum is in. There is no way she can give you more money. Instead of trying to keep up with Rupert, take pride in what you do have, and remember Rupert thinks you are pretty cool without all the expensive gear.

I FEEL LIKE AN OUTCAST

Elaine and Danielle, both 14, have been best friends since the start of secondary school. Elaine is quite shy and spends most of her time with Danielle. But lately, Danielle has started spending her breaks with a different group...

I've always been quite shy and find it hard to make friends. That's why I was so thrilled to meet Danielle. We totally hit it off – we both like horses – and spent every break-time with each other.

The only downside has been that we live quite a long way away from each other. Anyway, when we went back to school in September, Danielle seemed different. I also wasn't able to find her at break-times. I didn't say anything at first, as I didn't want to seem sad, but then it really started to bug me. I came straight out and asked her if she'd gone off me. She said that of course she hadn't, but during the summer she'd started hanging out with these girls who live in the next street to her. I just feel so hurt. I don't want to share Danielle with anybody.

> 'I just feel so hurt. I don't want to share Danielle with anybody.'

ASK THE EXPERTS...

Simon the social worker says...
When a close friendship cools it can be a major loss. Feeling sad is normal. You need time to pick yourself up. While you're feeling low you're vulnerable to being picked on and bullied by people who enjoy that sort of thing. So you might feel you ought to rush into new friendships. It's probably better to take the time to identify others you might want to be friends with – people with similar interests to you.

Anita the counsellor says...
It sounds like you're a positive person who had plenty of friends at primary school. It's hard to lose a friend and when people are cruel, it gets you down. It could be helpful to share your feelings with someone in your family who you are close to, or a teacher at school. Hard times don't last forever and if you start accepting invitations you will be on the way to being your old happy self again.

Mac the family liaison officer says...
Loneliness is a horrible emotion. It is even worse if people are picking on you. The first thing you need to tell yourself is that you don't deserve to be picked on, and that you shouldn't have to put up with it. Tell your parents and a teacher to get the bullying to stop. Secondly, why not say yes the next time anyone asks you out. They might not turn into a best friend, but being part of a group will make things a lot easier at school.

THE OUTCOMES

After reading our experts' advice, Natalie, Dan and Elaine wrote back to let us know how things turned out...

GET CONNECTED

FOLLOW THIS WEB LINK TO FIND OUT MORE:

www.teengrowth.com

A health website that offers information and advice on **puberty**, family, friends, drugs, sex and emotions.

C A S E   S T U D Y   1

Value yourself

After a lot of hard thinking and chatting things through with my mum, I realize that I have been out of order. Louise has always been a good friend to me, and she deserves better. I know that Louise gets all the attention from the boys at the moment, but instead of getting angry about this, I decided to tell her how I feel. She told me that some of the boys who had been hanging around her were asking about me! I feel really silly now. She has fixed me up with a really fit boy, and we are going out together on a double date next week!

C A S E   S T U D Y   2

Think it through

I feel bad about feeling envious of Rupert and his money. Obviously I wish I could afford to buy the kind of clothes he wears, but I know how hard Mum works and I know there is no way I can expect the kind of allowance Rupert gets. I'm going to carry on hanging out with Rupert and his friends but try not to compete anymore.

C A S E   S T U D Y   3

Time to move on

I've realized that although Danielle shouldn't have been distant with me, I need to take control of my own life. It was unrealistic to expect to be able to have one person totally to myself, and wrong to feel envious of Danielle making new friends. I spoke to Mum about things and she said the best thing to do is follow Danielle's example and make a new circle of friends. I have joined the netball team, and I really get on well with a couple of the girls. Now I'm not so dependent on Danielle I feel much happier about things.

REMEMBER
- If you are feeling jealous, try and think about your own qualities and what a good person you are.
- Jealousy and envy should never get in the way of a friendship. Talk to a friend if you are feeling this way towards them.
- Never take your own insecurities out on somebody else.

BLOW YOUR TOP

HOW TO DEAL WITH ANGER

Anger is a normal, healthy emotion. Getting angry motivates us to sort out a problem or right a wrong. Many injustices in life have been resolved because someone was riled enough to do something about it.

7 SAFE WAYS TO LET OUT YOUR ANGER

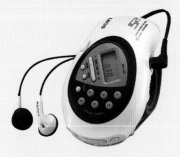

1 PUT ON YOUR FAVOURITE CD,
turn up the volume and dance madly around your bedroom!

2 GO SOMEWHERE WHERE YOU CAN BE ALONE
(and where you won't disturb anyone) and yell at the top of your lungs.

3 PUNCH A PILLOW

4 GO FOR A WALK,
a swim or kick a football around.

5 TRY WRITING IN A DIARY
or write a letter to the person you are angry with. You may work your anger out through the writing and not even have to send it!

6 TRY DISTRACTING YOURSELF FROM YOUR ANGRY FEELINGS
by putting on a video or reading a book or magazine.

7 ONCE YOU'VE SIMMERED DOWN A BIT,
try talking to someone about what made you angry.

We also get angry to protect ourselves or our loved ones from harm.

'Sometimes I get so angry I feel as though I need to punch a wall or something.'

If someone were hurting your brother or sister, you would be angry enough to jump to his or her defence, even if that person was twice your size! If you feel you are not being listened to, or that you have been misunderstood – it's perfectly natural to feel angry about it. And sometimes raising your voice is the only way to be heard so you can get your feelings off your chest. But if you feel angry all the time, or if it boils over and leads you to behave in a destructive way towards others or yourself, it's time to take a long hard look at what's going on in your head and sort it out.

Everyone expresses their emotions differently. Some people bottle up their frustrations, others release their feelings through crying. There are also some amongst us who feel that the only way to deal with the inner turmoil is to get angry with someone else. Anger is never constructive when it's expressed as violence. It is also unlikely that a situation that makes you unhappy will be resolved through shouting at someone. If these have been your strategies in the past, now's a good time to think of some other ways of dealing with the fire in your belly.

'Anyone can become angry – that's easy.
But to be angry with the right person, to the
right degree, at the right time, for the right
purpose and in the right way – that's not easy.'
(Aristotle, Greek philosopher)

TALK, DON'T SHOUT – TIPS ON EXPRESSING YOURSELF ... CALMLY

TRY NOT TO SHOUT
Raising your voice will only make the other
person scared or angry too.

TRY NOT TO CRITICISE
Avoid accusing the other person, because no one
likes to be told what they have done wrong.
Try saying, 'When you [do/say] such-and-such,
it makes me feel angry' – that way you are
owning the feelings rather than fixing blame.

LISTEN TO THE OTHER PERSON
Everyone has the right to air their views.
If you want someone to listen to your thoughts,
you need to be prepared to listen to theirs.

NO NEED TO BE DEFENSIVE
Don't be afraid to show your feelings.
It's okay to cry or admit that you
feel upset, wronged or left out.

MY BROTHERS DRIVE ME MAD

Emma, 14, gets annoyed when her older brothers make too much noise and keep her awake at night. She gets so riled about it that she ends up being too angry to get to sleep!

> 'They've just got no consideration and they just think of themselves.

Often my brothers are still up when I go to bed and they always argue over what's on TV.

They always have it loud, too, and I need quiet to go to sleep. It makes me so angry. They've just got no consideration and they only think of themselves. But if I get out of bed and shout at them they just laugh and that makes me even more mad and then I'm just so fuming I can't sleep at all.

Even if they turn the TV off and go to bed I'm just left lying there, fuming. They really have no respect for anyone but themselves. Sometimes I hate being the only girl in the family!

ASK THE EXPERTS...

Simon the social worker says...
Getting stressed from your brothers' noise is the last thing you need at bedtime. There's no obvious way to get rid of your anger and get a good night's sleep. As you said, it's about consideration and respect. It's also about rules and who's in charge. Therefore, let other people in your family – like your parents – know about your brothers' attitude problem.

Anita the counsellor says...
You are outnumbered by your brothers, which doesn't help your situation. Lying awake at night fuming is affecting no one but yourself so try a relaxation technique to help you switch off – visualize yourself lying on a beach while the waves lap the shore. If talking to your brothers in the calm light of day doesn't help, that's probably the time to enlist some parental support.

Mac the family liaison officer says...
Ask your parents to sort this out. Meanwhile, buy yourself some earplugs. You need some 'consideration rules' at home, like keeping the TV low when someone is trying to sleep. Try to keep things in perspective: thank them when they make an effort to be quiet. Perhaps you could make your point by going to bed early and getting up early, so you can wake them up and tell them what a lovely morning it is?

HE'S ALWAYS THE CRITIC

Ed, 14, gets mad with his stepfather for telling him what to do all the time. Ed feels as though he can never do anything right and worries that one day he's going to lose his rag completely.

> 'He'll make me do things and then say I didn't do it right and then he'll make me do it again.'

My stepdad makes me angry because he's really **patronising** and thinks he can boss me about all the time.

He'll make me do things and then say I didn't do it right and then he'll make me do it again. I don't say anything to him, I just stomp around looking fed up. He can tell I'm annoyed without me saying anything. I'm worried that just one day I'm going to blow and that will really upset my mum. But really, it's not his right to tell me what to do – especially not in such a rude and patronising way. It's not like I've got a hang-up about him taking my father-figure role or anything. He's been with my mum for ages and I'm used to having him around. I think he just likes to throw his weight around and unfortunately for me, I'm his target!

ASK THE EXPERTS...

Simon the social worker says...
Life gets complicated when someone new joins a family. It's even worse if they come in and start telling you what to do. Perhaps you and your stepdad got off on the wrong foot with each other. Or maybe that's just his style of dealing with people? Try telling him what you think is happening when you can talk about it calmly. Let off steam with friends if you need to. Talk to another adult in the family if nothing changes.

Anita the counsellor says...
Your stepdad may not be aware of how his behaviour is making you feel. Have you tried showing him how mature you are by talking to him about your feelings and how you would prefer to be treated? If this is too daunting or falls on deaf ears perhaps you could talk to your mum before you lose your temper and cause a family crisis. She may be able to mediate on your behalf and get your stepdad to ease up on you.

Mac the family liaison officer says...
Sometimes when you're really angry, it helps to write down what you want. Then you can either give your stepdad the note or read it out to him. That should help you stay in control and stop you saying more than is wise. It would be even better if you can balance your comments and say what you think he is doing well, or what you are prepared to do to help the situation. It's just as hard being a stepdad as a 14-year-old!

I'M TOO COMPETITIVE

Raj, 14, finds it impossible to keep his cool when he's on the court. If he misses a shot he can't help himself from swearing and smashing his racket on the ground.

'My dad's refused to play with me anymore because I get so foul-mouthed.'

I love sport and play whatever, whenever I can. Mostly I play football and I'm in the school team.

That's okay. I don't get angry on the pitch, even if I mess up. I guess there is no time to be angry. It's when I play badminton or tennis that I get really angry. I get so frustrated that I throw my racket down or smash the ball or just swear really badly. My dad's refused to play with me anymore because I get so foul-mouthed. I just can't help it though. I suppose my problem is that I'm just too **competitive.** Sport's really important to me and I just have really high standards for myself. I push myself really, really hard and give myself a really hard time when I don't play at my best.

ASK THE EXPERTS...

Simon the social worker says...
There's a big difference between team games where everyone works together to win and sports that are all about individual strength and skill. So don't be too hard on yourself about being competitive. Perhaps you're more of a team player at heart. And maybe you need to have more fun with your dad and less of a workout!

Anita the counsellor says...
It's interesting that you do have the skill to do this on the football pitch even when you are frustrated with yourself. How do you manage this? Is there anything that works that you can transfer to racquet sports? Maybe it's worth talking to your dad about how much you enjoy playing sports with him and see if you can enlist his support in gaining control. Bringing your sense of humour along could be really helpful!

Mac the family liaison officer says...
Try more sports that are not competitive. Work through your **angst** by trampolining or distance swimming. Try and work out what the 'fuse' is that starts your anger and avoid it. Make yourself take a deep breath and look at an alternative scenario for each angry outburst, e.g. Instead of 'I am so stupid for missing that ball', think: 'I couldn't reach that ball because I was in the wrong position'.

THE OUTCOMES

After reading our experts' advice, Emma, Ed and Raj wrote back to let us know how things turned out.

CASE STUDY 1

Know when to **compromise**

I got my parents involved and told them I was so tired at school that I couldn't concentrate. **That made them do something about it.** They told my brothers to stop being so inconsiderate and my brothers HAD to listen to them. My brothers gave me a hard time but I didn't care because they shouldn't have been so selfish. Mum did tell me that they couldn't all go round walking on tiptoes because I was trying to get to sleep, so she gave me some earplugs!

CASE STUDY 2

Speak your mind

I did blow. He pushed me too far one day and I was just so angry it all came out. I was really swearing at him and then I stormed out of the house. When I'd calmed down, I did regret it a bit. I didn't know what to do or where to go. Mum called me on my mobile and told me to get home. Mum and I had a talk. She wasn't angry but she was upset. I heard mum and my stepdad having an argument that night and that made me feel a bit guilty, but things have gone back to normal now. He's still **patronising** but I've said my piece and I'm glad.

CASE STUDY 3

Don't lose your rag

I tried explaining to my dad that I find it really hard to control my anger when we play. He said that it's no excuse to use such bad language and I guess he's right. I want to control my temper because I like playing sport with Dad. Deep breaths and counting to ten are kind of helping.

GET CONNECTED

FOLLOW THESE WEB LINKS TO FIND OUT MORE:

www.youngminds.org.uk/ youngpeople

A website dedicated to looking after the mental health of young people. Good for information on everything from **anxiety** to **depression**.

www.kidscape.org.uk

Kidscape is a national charity set up to protect children from bullying and harm. It has good articles on making friends and starting a new school.

REMEMBER

- Take some deep breaths and count to ten before you respond to whatever has made you angry.
- No one is going to respect your opinion if you are yelling or violent.
- Try going to your room and writing down your feelings before you confront the source of your anger.
- You need to find a healthy **outlet** for anger. Talking when you are calm is always the best option.
- Listen to the other person. If you both air your views, you should be able to reach a **compromise**.

BODY LANGUAGE: SIGNS OF ATTRACTION

HOW DO YOU KNOW WHEN SOMEONE FANCIES YOU?

- They start whispering to their friends and looking your way whenever you're around.

- They hassle you loads.

- They always seem to end up near you – on the bus or in the playground.

- They give you a present or card. Or go out of their way to do nice things for you.

- He/she is suddenly interested in what you're into.

- They ask your opinion – 'do you like my new jacket?' or 'what do you think of dance music?'

LOVE BUG

FALLING HEAD OVER HEELS

Chances are you've met or seen someone before that has made your heart flip. Butterflies in the stomach, dizziness, can't think about anything else – all these feelings are triggered by a mass release of hormones that comes with being a teenager.

We've met some of these hormones before, but there are also new hormones that cause a whole breed of strange emotions.

These are the 'sex hormones', which turn you from child into adult, able to make and have babies. These hormones are responsible for the sudden switch from feeling that the opposite sex is not worth your time to suddenly being interested!

'It's so weird. I've completely lost my appetite and all I can think about is her. I guess I must be in love.'

It's a fun, exciting and interesting time – a whole new world of crushes, **flirtations** and gossip opens up. This is the time when you find out what attracts you to someone; how to attract the people you like; and how to deal with the intense emotions that come with liking or loving someone. But along with love comes **heartache** and a certain amount of responsibility for other people's feelings. It's tough if you've got a crush on someone and the subject of your desire doesn't want to know. It can knock your confidence. But everyone experiences knocks at some time in their lives – the trick is knowing how to get over it and move on.

The only way to learn about how to maintain a long-lasting, healthy relationship where you connect on many levels is to keep trying.

Some people might feel disadvantaged in the dating stakes – perhaps you're not as good-looking, funny or smart as your mates. But remember this, everyone has something special to offer. Your first job is to find out what your unique qualities are and then project them to the world. Everyone feels unsure and awkward about dating at first. Finding true love is a life-enriching thing though, and it won't happen unless you put yourself out there and try.

'After I broke up with my boyfriend, I was gutted for ages.'

5 WAYS TO DEAL WITH A KNOCK-BACK

1 TALK TO SOMEONE ABOUT HOW YOU FEEL

2 CRY, SCREAM, WRITE POETRY
Do whatever you've got to do in your own time.

3 HOLD A SPECIAL CEREMONY TO BID FAREWELL TO THE RELATIONSHIP
Write him/her a letter explaining your feelings then dig a hole and bury it, along with a photo of you together.

4 RETAIL THERAPY ALWAYS HELPS

5 ORGANIZE A DAY OUT WITH YOUR FRIENDS
You never know, you might even spot some new talent.

PSYCHO GIRL

Kelly-Ann, 14, has strong feelings for a boy in her class but hasn't been able to pluck up the courage to talk to him. Now his friends are giving her a really hard time and she feels humiliated.

I'm completely obsessed with this boy, Nic, in my class. I think about him all the time and write his name everywhere.

My friends really encouraged me to talk to him and so I'd kind of follow him around trying to find an opportunity to pluck up courage to say something to him. Then his friends got really funny about it and kept saying to him, 'Oh look, Nic, there's your stalker again' or, 'Here comes the psycho'. It was really awful. Then one of them phoned me up pretending to be Nic, saying he really fancied me. I knew it wasn't him. I feel really stupid and humiliated. I just really like him, that's all, but I guess I haven't gone about it in a very smart way. My friends think the whole thing is funny, but I can't see it that way – it's put me off boys for life!

> 'I'd kind of follow him around trying to find an opportunity to pluck up courage to say something to him.'

ASK THE EXPERTS...

Simon the social worker says...
It sounds as though the boy you're imagining might be a far nicer guy than the real thing. You know – you could just keep him as your secret dream boy. Or, if after everything that's happened, you think you can be brave and try talking to him, then go for it! What have you got to lose? If he turns out to be a jerk, then at least you know you've given it your best shot and you can move on and look for someone else.

Anita the counsellor says...
The strong feelings you have for Nic are completely normal at your age. Because your friends and his are still learning about how to handle attraction, they haven't been very mature in this situation which has left you feeling stupid. I would be very surprised if you are put off boys for the rest of your life. Maybe you have learnt something from this about being more cautious in sharing your feelings in the future.

Mac the family liaison officer says...
Sometimes, going through an embarrassment like this helps to put things in perspective. Next time, try to be cool and friendly without going 'over the top'. Your friends probably think it's funny because they've done the same thing. You'll know how to handle it better next time.

HOW DO I GET OUT OF IT?

Kev, 14, is stuck in a relationship he's not happy with. He likes Jaz as a person and wants to break up with her without hurting her feelings.

I asked this girl, Jaz, out a few months ago and everything I'd first liked about her started to get on my nerves.

I've been wanting to break up with her for weeks but I don't know how to do it or what to say. We hardly see each other and when we do it's all really weird and strained. One of my mates says I should just tell her I don't fancy her anymore. Another mate says I should go off with this other girl who likes me, but I like Jaz and I don't want to make her look bad or hurt her.

'Everything I'd first liked about her started to get on my nerves.'

ASK THE EXPERTS...

Simon the social worker says...
All new relationships change over time. Explain to Jaz how you feel in a way that isn't hurtful. It's to your credit that you don't want to hurt her. But you could hurt her by leaving her hanging on, so it's best to just be honest. Suggest remaining friends if you are both happy with that scenario.

Anita the counsellor says...
You sound like a pretty mature, considerate kind of guy. Sometimes, when we're first starting out with dating, we can misinterpret our own feelings for another person — or someone else comes along and our feelings for the first person change or disappear. The important thing is to be honest with yourself and with your girlfriend. If she's a nice person, she should understand and still want to be friends.

Mac the family liaison officer says...
It's quite natural at your age to be 'testing' people and relationships. The important thing is to handle the break tactfully so that neither of you feels humiliated and you can still be friends. She probably feels the relationship is strained and finds it as uncomfortable as you do. Be honest, but be kind. Just tell her how it is. I'm sure she would prefer that to being two-timed.

HE WON'T TALK TO ME

Rosie, 14, met a cute boy at a school disco and her mates gave him her mobile number. Now she keeps getting phone calls where the person on the other end doesn't say anything.

I met a boy at a school disco a while ago. I've seen him around town and he seems really nice, but he's quite shy.

It was fine at the disco because he was with his mates and I was with mine, so everyone was talking to everyone else. Some of my friends are really mouthy and they gave him my mobile number because they knew I liked him.

The annoying thing is that I think he keeps calling me, but he never says anything. There's this geek from my old school who keeps calling me too, so it could just be him (and I really DON'T like him), but if it is the boy I fancy, how can I

> 'The annoying thing is that I think he keeps calling me, but he never says anything.'

make him talk to me? I'm shy too, so if I see him in town, I can't go up to him. I just dash into a shop and watch him until he's out of sight.

ASK THE EXPERTS...

Simon the social worker says...
There's no way you can make someone talk to you! Perhaps your mates could help out by delivering messages on your behalf, getting his number so you can text him, or by being with you when you see him and his mates. Create opportunities where you both feel more comfortable.

Anita the counsellor says...
It's really helpful being able to meet people when you are in a group. That way you can all get to know each other without too much pressure. It must be frustrating not knowing if you're being called by the boy of your dreams or of your nightmares though! I would suggest that you risk a smile if you see him when you're out on your own. If that's too scary, are your mouthy mates up for a bit of matchmaking?

Mac the family liaison officer says...
It sounds as if you're quite similar in temperament and would get on well. Try to meet a few more times when you both have groups of friends around to support you. Perhaps your friends could suggest a bowling trip, or a trip to another disco where you can gradually get to know each other better without too much pressure.

THE OUTCOMES

After reading our experts' advice, Kelly-Ann, Kev and Rosie wrote back to let us know how things turned out.

CASE STUDY 1

Ease off a bit

His friends have just about stopped embarrassing me and I don't talk about him anymore with my friends. I still go all funny when I see him, but he's going out with someone else and that's that. I feel a real fool so I'm going to play it cool the next time I fancy someone.

CASE STUDY 2

Don't give up

I managed to find the courage to tell Jaz I didn't want to see her anymore. She said, 'Phew, thank God for that!' She was really relieved! Apparently she'd hoped it would just fizzle out because she didn't know how to tell me she'd gone off me. We actually had a laugh about it and we're still good mates, which I'm glad about because I don't hate her or anything. It was funny because I was partly relieved but part of me thought, 'What do you mean you don't like me anymore?' So much for my huge ego!

CASE STUDY 3

A little help from your friends

I've got a date and I'm really excited. It was all my mouthy mates' doing. One of them asked one of his friends whether he liked me and then she just marched up to him in town, put my phone number in his hand and said, 'Look, if you like her, ask her out. She won't say no.' I died! He went bright red. He didn't call for ages, but then he did and I could hardly speak. I went all giggly and stupid, but he asked if I wanted to go to the movies and I managed to control my voice to say, 'Yes, I'd love to.' And that's it. Not so bad after all!

REMEMBER
- It's completely natural to have feelings of attraction for others, even though it might feel weird at first.
- You might feel shy or uncomfortable about approaching someone you fancy. Try asking a mate to approach them on your behalf.
- A break-up might feel like the end of the world, but in all sincerity – you will survive.
- The most important thing to remember is to relax and BE YOURSELF.

GET CONNECTED

FOLLOW THESE WEB LINKS TO FIND OUT MORE:

www.teengrowth.com

A health website that offers information and gives advice on **puberty**, sex and emotions.

www.bbc.co.uk/teens

This BBC website is an excellent teen site covering everything from entertainment to life issues.

A FEW SHORT STEPS TO INSTANT HAPPINESS...

Get enough sleep
Sleep deprivation makes you grouchy and stressed.

Exercise
Exercise not only gives you energy but also helps stimulate the body's endorphins (or happy hormones).

Eat well
You are what you eat. Your body and mind function best on a healthy, balanced diet. The less 'processed' the food, the better. Limit fast food and fizzy drinks.

Drink water
A couple of litres a day is recommended, but if you don't drink lots of water now, try to build this up slowly.

Communicate
If something bugs you, talk about it. If you have a problem, tell someone.

Find a bit of 'me time' every day
Think about what you want to achieve during these special times and make plans. TV is fine, but there's a lot of life to be had out there — don't let it pass you by!

LOTS TO SMILE ABOUT

PUT ON A HAPPY FACE

Happiness is the very best of emotions and it is a state we all want to be in most of the time.

Along with all the difficulties **puberty** throws at you, your teenage years can be a time when you have new freedoms, special friendships and a lot of fun. As long as the happy times outweigh the not-so-happy times, you should come out the other side laughing.

Joy is a strong and immediate emotion that makes you want to jump, shout, dance or generally behave like a crazy person. No doubt you've felt joy at some time in your life. It's a great feeling.

'I love laughing so much my tummy hurts!'

42

Hold on to it and remember when things aren't so good. So what is the secret to happiness? Being loved and loving others? Having lots of money? Football? Well, the secret is … there is no secret! Happiness is different things for different people. No doubt you know the things that make you smile or feel warm inside. If only you could capture that feeling, hang on to the moment when you felt carefree and couldn't stop grinning from ear to ear – so you could just switch it on whenever things didn't seem so rosy. But the reality is, there would be no 'happy' without 'sad'. Everything needs an opposite – that's just nature.

WHAT MAKES YOU HAPPY?

NADIA, 15

My little sister who's nine makes me really happy. She loves spending time with me and I like the fact that I can teach her stuff. That makes me feel good about myself.

ED, 14

A good day at school followed by hanging out and biking or skateboarding. Having a laugh with friends and winding people up!

BEN, 15

I'm really **competitive**, so whenever I do well at something or beat someone else - it gives me a real buzz. I do lots of sport and if we've had a good match I feel really good.

BRIDY, 15

I love it when everyone in the family is happy, everything is going well and we've got stuff to look forward to, like a holiday or something. And I love it when I've got money and can go shopping with my friends.

FIERY, LOVED-UP OR SCAREDY CAT?

Stretch out on the therapist's couch and discover what kind of person you are with this probing personality quiz.

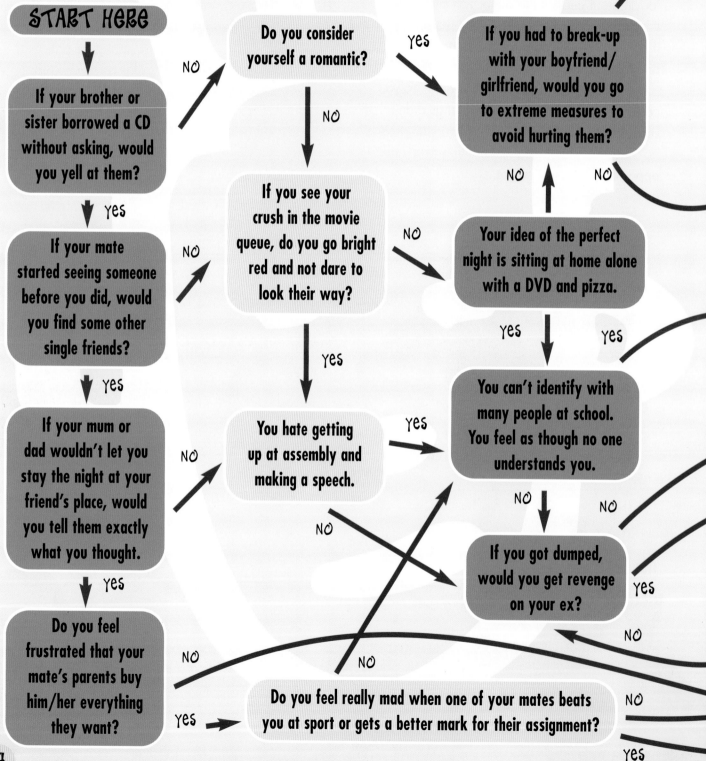

START HERE

If your brother or sister borrowed a CD without asking, would you yell at them?

NO

yes

If your mate started seeing someone before you did, would you find some other single friends?

yes

If your mum or dad wouldn't let you stay the night at your friend's place, would you tell them exactly what you thought.

yes

Do you feel frustrated that your mate's parents buy him/her everything they want?

NO

yes

Do you consider yourself a romantic?

NO

NO

yes

If you see your crush in the movie queue, do you go bright red and not dare to look their way?

NO

yes

You hate getting up at assembly and making a speech.

yes

NO

If you had to break-up with your boyfriend/girlfriend, would you go to extreme measures to avoid hurting them?

NO

NO

Your idea of the perfect night is sitting at home alone with a DVD and pizza.

yes

yes

You can't identify with many people at school. You feel as though no one understands you.

NO

NO

If you got dumped, would you get revenge on your ex?

yes

NO

Do you feel really mad when one of your mates beats you at sport or gets a better mark for their assignment?

NO

yes

44

yes

yes

OVERFLOWING WITH LOVE

You are very emotionally mature for your years! Your mates are lucky to have such a kind and thoughtful friend in you. You will always stand up for what you believe is right, yet still remain conscious not to cause offence to anyone. Sounds like you are ready to start dating – and no doubt there will be lots of fit teens sending you Valentines because you've certainly got that X-Factor – warmth, generosity and a great big heart!

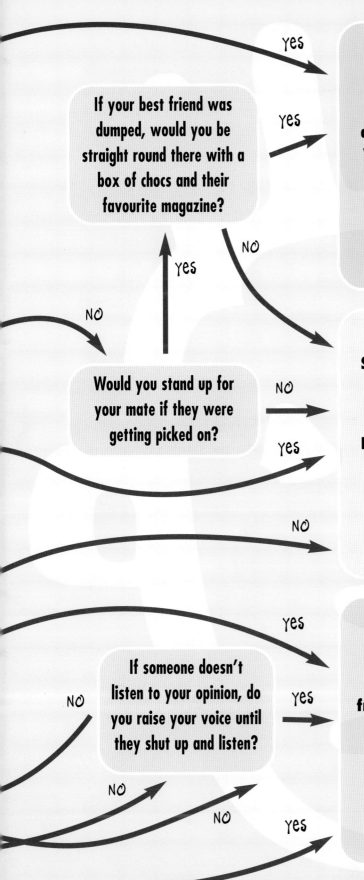

If your best friend was dumped, would you be straight round there with a box of chocs and their favourite magazine?

yes

NO

yes

NO

Would you stand up for your mate if they were getting picked on?

NO

MAKE AN EFFORT TO MINGLE

Sounds like socializing might not come so easy to you. That's okay. Some of us are naturally more attracted to the limelight than others. You might be more into your own company or perhaps you are just downright shy! Whatever the reason, chances are you're not as happy as you might be – because everyone needs support from others in some shape or form. Communication is your most useful tool, even if you have to force yourself to speak up.

yes

NO

yes

If someone doesn't listen to your opinion, do you raise your voice until they shut up and listen?

NO

yes

NO

NO

yes

YOU NEED TO CHILL OUT!

You better try controlling that fiery temper if you want a smooth ride into adulthood. What are the qualities you look for in a friendship, and what are the things that people see in you? Are they attracted by your tough exterior? Revenge might be sweet but resentment and jealousy will only make you feel constantly grumpy and bitter. And as for dating – most people are looking for a kind person to get close to, not someone who's going to spread rumours if you break up!

ADRENALINE *hormone released in response to stress or fear*

ALTERNATIVE THERAPIES *health treatments that use natural ingredients rather than chemical medicines. Examples include aromatherapy (which uses special plant oils) and homeopathy (which uses herbs and minerals).*

ANGST *strong feeling of anxiety about life*

ANTI-DEPRESSANTS *drugs, such as the well-known Prozac, that are prescribed by a doctor for depression and anxiety disorders*

ANXIETY *a heightened feeling of worry or stress*

APPREHENSIVE *worried or afraid about what might happen*

COMPETITIVE *wanting to be more successful than others*

COMPROMISE *an agreement made by both sides where both meet somewhere in the middle*

DEFENSIVE *very eager to avoid being criticised or blamed*

DEPRESSION *feeling of hopelessness or unhappiness that doesn't shift*

ENDORPHINS *group of hormones that lift your mood*

FLIRTATION *trying to attract someone you like in a playful way*

HEARTACHE *grief – often caused by a break-up or other kind of big loss*

HORMONES *substances in the body that stimulate parts of your body (including feelings) into action*

INFERIOR *not as important as other things or people*

INSECURITY COMPLEX *constant feelings of not being as good as everyone else and feeling bad about yourself*

MEDITATION *relaxing technique that involves sitting still, closing your eyes and focusing your thoughts on one simple thing, like your breathing*

OUTLET *way or method of expressing your inner feelings*

PARANOID *feeling worried about what people think of you, in a way that's irrational or unreasonable*

PATRONISING *treating someone as if they are not as important as yourself*

PHOBIA *extreme fear of one particular thing, e.g. spiders, heights or fear of the dark*

PUBERTY *the period when teenagers reach sexual maturity*

SELF-CONSCIOUS *nervous or awkward about how you come across to others*

SELF-ESTEEM *confidence in your own worth or abilities*

TRANSITION *process of changing from one state to another*

THE GET REAL ADVICE DIRECTORY

If you've got a problem and you'd like to talk to a trained professional or counsellor, here are some useful numbers. Don't suffer in silence. These helplines are there to help you and you don't have to give your name.

HELPLINES

ANTI-BULLYING CAMPAIGN 0207 381446
Advice on anything to do with bullying.

CHILDLINE 0800 1111
www.childline.org.uk
For help with any worries or problems.

KIDSCAPE 08451 205204
www.kidscape.org.uk
For help with bullying or abuse.

NSPCC 0808 8005000
www.worriedneed2talk.org.uk
A free counselling and advice line.

THE LINE 0800 2797454
Free counselling for teenagers.

THE SAMARITANS 08457 909090
www.samaritans.org
For help with any worries or problems.

YOUTH 2 YOUTH 020 88963675
Emotional advice from young people.

OTHER ORGANIZATIONS

AUSTRALIAN DRUG FOUNDATION
www.adf.org.au
The Australian Drug Foundation has a wide range of information on all aspects of drugs, their effects and their legal position in Australia.

CRUSE BEREAVEMENT
www.rd4u.org.co.uk
Confidential advice for those dealing with the death of a close friend or family member.

DRINKWISE
www.drinkwise.co.uk
Advice on anything to do with alcohol.

EATING DISORDERS ASSOCIATION 0845 6347650
www.edauk.com
For those people suffering from an eating disorder, or their friends and family.

FRANK 0800 776600
www.talktofrank.com
For free and confidential advice about drugs and smoking (formerly the National Drugs Helpline).

GET CONNECTED 0808 8084994
www.getconnected.org.uk
For anyone who's run away or been thrown out of their home.

LGBT YOUTHLINE 0845 1130005
Support and advice for gay young people or those confused about their sexuality.

NATIONAL AIDS HELPLINE 0800 567123
For help and advice about AIDS or HIV.

NATIONAL MISSING PERSONS HELPLINE 0500 700700
www.missingpersons.org
Help for the families of missing persons.

RAPE CRISIS 0115 9003560
Support for rape sufferers.

RELATEEN 0845 4561310
For young people wanting to talk about family problems or relationships.